T0128425

EXPERIENCING OUR *Extraordinary God* IN OUR ORDINARY LIVES

DEBBIE HENN

WESTBOW
PRESS®
A DIVISION OF THOMAS NELSON
& ZONDERVAN

WestBow Press books may be ordered through booksellers or by contacting:

WestBow Press
A Division of Thomas Nelson & Zondervan
1663 Liberty Drive
Bloomington, IN 47403
www.westbowpress.com
844-714-3454

Scripture quotations are taken from The Holy Bible, English Standard Version® (ESV®), Copyright © 2001 by Crossway, a publishing ministry of Good News Publishers. All rights reserved.

Interior Image Credit: Anna Dickson

ISBN: 978-1-6642-8344-2 (sc)
ISBN: 978-1-6642-8343-5 (e)

Library of Congress Control Number: 2022920850

Print information available on the last page.

WestBow Press rev. date: 12/08/2022

The LORD your God is in your midst,
a mighty one who will save;
he will rejoice over you with gladness;
he will quiet you by his love;
he will exult over you with loud singing.
—Zephaniah 3:17

To all those who have knowingly or unknowingly
taught me the truth and led me to
God the Father,
God the Son,
God the Holy Spirit.

To God be the glory.

PREFACE

I have always been drawn to the idea of God. I wanted to know about Him, but my understanding was very limited.

I believed what I heard and learned in church—that God is love and that Jesus came into this world to save and rescue sinners. I was twelve years old when I heard, and I believed. It would be many more years before I knew and understood that it was possible to have a relationship with Jesus and that the Holy Spirit could and would change my life.

Through a series of testimonies, scriptures, Bible studies, and praise music, I heard Jesus call me to learn about and follow Him. I said yes, and I have never looked back. I did not follow because of anything in myself other than a conviction that Jesus was my only hope for redemption, salvation, and eternal life. I have stumbled and fallen many times. Every time I've stumbled, God was right there by me to pick me up and draw me closer to Him.

I began to set aside a time early in the morning to read a devotional book and study the Bible. During this time I began to keep a journal of my daily life, as well as what I was learning from scripture. The two were intertwined. When I was writing in my journal, I would get an idea from my ordinary life that reminded me of a spiritual truth I had learned.

These stories are the spiritual truths I have seen in my ordinary life. Each thought and story spoke to me about an extraordinary God who I wanted to know better.

My prayer is that you will also experience our extraordinary God in your ordinary life.

THE CAMELLIA BUSH

When we lived in Louisiana, I planted a camellia bush in my back yard. I had seen pictures of beautiful camellia blossoms, and I was looking forward to having some of my very own. My bush was tucked away in a corner where only a few people could see it, but I knew right where it was. When I thought it was time for it to bloom, I began to check daily for blossoms. The buds were plentiful, but there were no flowers.

After many weeks of waiting and watching, I walked out one day to find that the camellia bush had bloomed and was filled with the most beautiful flowers. I was surprised and delighted.

In that moment I came to understand that it had simply been a late bloomer, and although it did not have a large audience to show off for, it had me, who found so much joy in its beauty.

I understand that I am like my camellia bush: my buds might last longer than others, but I will bloom at just the right time. I need to also remember that I have an audience of one who watches over me and celebrates when I bloom.

Lord, I pray that I will bear the fruit you have destined for me. I humbly ask for the patience I need to bloom in your time.

I need to remember that "He has made everything beautiful in its time" (Ecclesiastes 3:11).

Reflection:

- In what ways have you been impatient with God's timing in your life?

- Consider writing a prayer asking God to teach you that He is working in your life and that, in Him, you and your circumstances will bloom at just the right time.

Ecclesiastes 3:11

GOD IS THE PERFECT PARENT

When our daughter was ready to walk, I was excited for this new development. I remember standing her up against the wall, getting down on her level, and encouraging her to walk to me. She stood there for a while, and I could tell she wanted to come to me but wasn't quite sure how to do it. She wobbled a bit, took a first step, and then fell down. I rushed to her, picked her up, hugged her, and said, "Let's try again." We did that many times until one day she took two steps, then three steps before falling down.

Next she began to take steps holding onto my hand or the coffee table. It was exciting as she began to walk with help and then toddled on her own.

Babies aren't born walking. They scoot on their tummies and then crawl and then, with much practice, they walk.

My walk with God has been like that. Each time I have taken a few steps and fallen down He has picked me up and lovingly let me try again. I have learned it is all part of a process. I want to live my life according to God's purposes, but I fail so many times. I don't hear words of condemnation; I hear words of forgiveness, mercy, and encouragement that allow me to try again. Each time I get closer to walking in God's ways, I know it pleases Him—just as I was pleased when my daughter was able to walk to me. God doesn't really ask me to do things perfectly; He asks me to try. He looks at my heart, and like the most caring, loving parent, He knows that His child is learning how to walk in His ways and is pleased with my effort.

> And so, from the day we heard, we have not ceased to pray for you, asking that you may be filled with the knowledge of his will in all spiritual wisdom and understanding, so as to walk in a manner worthy of the Lord, fully pleasing to him: bearing fruit in every good work and increasing in the knowledge of God; being strengthened with all power, according to his glorious might, for all endurance and patience with joy; giving thanks to the Father, who has qualified you to share in the inheritance of the saints in light. (Colossians 1:9–12)

Reflection:

- Take a moment and talk to your heavenly Father about the times you believe you failed. Let Him speak words of love and encouragement to you.

THE STORM

To celebrate my granddaughter's fifth-grade graduation, she hiked the Appalachian Trail section called the Presidential Traverse with a group of her friends and their dads. The Presidential Traverse is known to be a difficult and strenuous hike, and storms often show up out of nowhere. On one of the last days of the hike, they were on the top of the mountain and headed toward a cabin where they would eat dinner with the rest of the group. Suddenly the sky turned black, and lightning was striking down all around them. The storm clouds lowered to the top of the mountain, making it difficult to see in front of them, and they lost all sense of direction. There was no shelter or trees—nowhere to take refuge. They were lost, vulnerable, and helpless.

They had not been far from their destination when the storm rolled in. Some in the group had already made it to the cabin. Seeing the dangerous storm and knowing that part of the group was still out there, one of the dad's ran out of the cabin, yelling into the storm to help them navigate their way to safety.

I often think of my granddaughter's experience on top of that mountain—and about the storms that have popped up unexpectedly in my own life. I have experienced a divorce, the death of my mother, regrets, and failures. In those times I felt lost and could not see the way forward. Although I could not navigate out of the storm on my own, I have a God who comes out calling for me and guiding me to his refuge. I am reminded time and time again of the following verses:

> But let all who take refuge in you rejoice;
> Let them ever sing for joy,
> and spread your protection over them,
> that those who love your name may exult in you.
> (Psalm 5:11)

> For you have been my refuge, a strong tower against the enemy. Let me dwell in your tent forever! Let me take refuge under the shelter of your wings! (Psalm 61:3–4)

Reflection:

- Where do you seek refuge from the storms in your life?

THE WORD
RECEIVE

W e have been taught it is better to give than to receive. But I believe that until we understand how to receive freely, we are unable to freely give to others.

In the chaos and celebration that December holds, I was often reminded of the joy of receiving through the experiences of my granddaughters. When they were little they would come to my house and help me place all the ornaments on my tree. I could feel their anticipation build as they decorated, imagining what would soon be under the tree for them.

In Matthew 19:14 Jesus says, "Let the little children come to me and do not hinder them, for the kingdom of heaven belongs to such as these."

I have come to understand this verse in its fullness through my grandchildren, because children understand the secret of receiving. They are naturally inclined to receive what is given to them with the fullness of joy.

God invites each of us to receive His great gifts like a child at Christmas who is filled with anticipation. His gifts of love, mercy, forgiveness and grace have no limits, and he freely and joyfully gives them to us. Out of that abundance, God gives us the opportunity to share these gifts with others so that they may know Him and His great love. I am able to love abundantly, accept others, forgive more freely and extend grace only through receiving the gifts that He has given to me.

"We love because He first loved us." (1 John 4:19)

"Blessed be the God and Father of our Lord Jesus Christ, the Father of mercies and God of all comfort, who comforts us in all our affliction, so that we may be able to comfort those who are in affliction, with the comfort with which we ourselves were comforted by God." (2 Corinthians 1:3–4)

Reflection:

- Can you recall a time in your life when you received love, mercy, forgiveness, or grace from someone? How did that experience shape you?

- Consider writing about a time when you were able to give someone else the gifts you have received of love, mercy, forgiveness, or grace.

1 John 4:19

SUKEY'S CATS

My sister, Sukey, had recently adopted two kittens and made plans for them to be neutered. We spoke on the eve of their surgery, and she remarked, as they joyfully played with reckless abandon, that they had no idea what was in store for them the following day.

In the morning they saw the carrier and were instantly afraid. They did not know that this situation was temporary, that they were not in danger, and that Sukey would be there to bring them home after the procedure to love and care for them.

The story of my sister's cats came to mind as I was in the midst of the holidays and making plans with our daughter while she was visiting.

I am a planner. I love to dream and prepare for the next week, month, and year. Uncertainty for me is always unsettling, and it's difficult at times to realize that I am much like Sukey's cats. I do not know what the next moment holds.

December 26 began as just another day. We took advantage of the unseasonably warm weather, went for a hike, and made plans to take a quick trip to Asheville, North Carolina, the following day. We ended the day with a piece of chocolate cake, and I was blissfully unaware that something was about to happen that would change my life.

My daughter noticed I was drooling after a bite of chocolate cake, and when she spoke to me, I was slurring my words. Immediately she and my husband knew I was having a stroke, and they called 911 so that I could get the quickest care possible. Meanwhile, I was in a twilight world. I could hear what was happening, but I didn't have the ability to fully understand or communicate.

During the next several days while I was in ICU, I dreamed that I heard God speak to me and say over and over again, "For I know the plans I have for you … plans for welfare and not for evil, to give you a future and a hope" (Jeremiah 29:11).

Those words gave me much comfort and hope.

As I continue my recovery and grow stronger every day, I am grateful that God is in control. I am able to trust that His plan will continue to work for my ultimate good. He will continue to love me and care for me in every circumstance I face.

Reflection:

- Have you been, or are you now, in a place where your plans have been interrupted? What was your response? Can you describe your feelings about that?

- Can you trust God's promise that His plans for you are for your welfare to give you a future and hope? What obstacles do you have for trusting God?

A TRANSPLANT

My brother-in-law, Jack, was very ill with cancer. He was being considered for a bone marrow transplant with the hope that this procedure would cure him. We all prayed for him to be given the gift of healing through this transplant.

As I prayed, I was struck with the thought that we are all in need of transplants. We need a spiritual transplant in order for us to be given the gift of eternal life. We must have Christ transplanted into our hearts.

Ezekiel 36:26 says, "And I will give you a new heart, and a new spirit I will put within you. And I will remove the heart of stone from your flesh and give you a heart of flesh."

We were devastated to learn that Jack was not eligible for the transplant as he was in the late stages of his disease; however, anyone who comes to Christ—no matter when, no matter where—and asks with faith to have His spirit transplanted in them will immediately receive the new spirit that is eternal life.

Jesus says, "Truly, Truly, I say to you, whoever hears my word and believes him who sent me has eternal life. He does not come into judgement, but has passed from death to life" (John 5:24).

Thank you, God, that I have nothing to fear. In Christ I have passed from death and judgment into eternal life.

Reflection:

- Have you experienced this new heart and new spirit? What does it feel like?

- If you have not experienced this new heart you can ask Jesus to give you His Spirit, which is eternal life.

YOKED TO CHRIST

I suffer from anxiety and sometimes feel anxious when I have no reason to. The feelings persist even without a rational source. These feelings can quickly overwhelm me, and then I am emotionally paralyzed. Sometimes the anxiety comes from a voice in my head that says things like, *You shouldn't have done that,* or *Why didn't you do that,* or *You aren't good enough.*

When caught in a whirlwind of anxiety, I remembered the scripture where Jesus says, "Come to me, all who labor and are heavy laden, and I will give you rest. Take my yoke upon you and learn from me; for I am gentle and lowly in heart and you will find rest for your souls. For my yoke is easy and my burden is light" (Matthew 11:28–30).

In thinking about this truth, I envisioned being yoked to Jesus. A yoke is used in order to make two animals walk closer together, and Jesus is asking me to be yoked to Him so that we can walk together.

In spite of all of my flaws, Jesus's deepest desire is to steadily walk by my side with a purpose while intimately showing me a new and better way of living. He guides and leads me into truth;

He carries my burdens; and He frees me from condemnation, accusations, and unrealistic expectations.

When I begin to wander off and put my trust, happiness, and self-worth in things like performing, the need to be noticed, the approval of another person, or the need to be in control, He gently pulls me back, because I am yoked to Him. He offers me rest for my soul.

Reflection:

- Have you found yourself, or are you now, yoked to something other than Jesus? What is it?

- Can you let that yoke go and become yoked to Jesus?

BLOOMING

We moved from the Midwest to the South, and I was amazed to learn people could plant flowers in the fall. I excitedly purchased pansies and snapdragons to plant in my new garden and waited with anticipation for them to bloom.

To my delight, the pansies bloomed right away and looked beautiful. The snapdragons, however, remained in little clumps of green throughout all of fall and winter.

I was disappointed as I compared the snapdragons' inaction to the pansies' continuous blooms and thought perhaps I'd planted them incorrectly, whether in location or timing. When spring arrived, I walked out to my garden, and much to my surprise, the snapdragons had bloomed and were *beautiful*. In that moment, I thought of Ecclesiastes 3:1, which says, "For everything there is a season, and a time for every matter under heaven."

I was struck with the thought that we are very much like the pansies and snapdragons in that we are created in a unique way and designed to bloom at different times, and no matter when we do, it is beautiful and breathtaking.

"Don't compare yourself to others. There is no comparison between the sun and the moon. They shine when it's their time." (Casey Ho)

Reflection:

- In what season of life do you find yourself right now?

- Do you find yourself comparing your situations or gifts to others?

- Ask God to show you how He has a purpose for your life and He compares you to no one.

For everything there is a season, and a time for every matter under heaven.

Ecclesiastes 3:1

GIFTS

love to buy little things for my granddaughters Sophie and Hazel.

When they were little, they would come to my house every Wednesday, and on some of those days I would have a little something special waiting for them. They were not expensive gifts, but rather little things I had seen that reminded me of them.

One Wednesday the older of the two, Sophie, who was four at the time, asked me, "Omi, did you buy something for me today?" as she looked around to see if there was anything new.

I replied that on this particular Wednesday I didn't have anything new waiting for her, but we used some time to reflect on gifts she had received on previous visits and played with those.

God loves to give us gifts too, and like Sophie, I find myself filled with anticipation as I await each one. His gifts can come to me in the form of squirrels running and playing in the yard, a cool breeze and shade on my walk, a letter from a friend, my perennial flowers coming back each spring, a day at the beach, or a song that turns my heart back to God.

I have learned that the blessings or gifts sometimes come through pain and into the darkness of my life. When I cannot see His gifts, I reflect on what He has already given me. Even in those dark moments, I am overwhelmed by God's love and the new mercies He brings to me every day!

> The steadfast love of the LORD never ceases;
> His mercies never come to an end;
> they are new every morning;
> great is your faithfulness. (Lamentations 3 :22–23)

Reflection:

- Make a list or journal the gifts and mercies you see and experience each day.

KITTENS

One day I saw a black cat in our backyard. She seemed to glance in my direction as she headed up to the woods. The next day my husband told me he had seen two kittens cuddled up asleep on the front porch. A black-and-white ball of fluff caught my eye as they ran off the porch when I peeked out the door.

We looked for the kittens and soon discovered a mom and three babies making their home under our back deck. We left out food and water for them and watched as their curiosity for the world began to grow. Even though we were providing food, water, and shelter for them, they were very afraid when they saw us—even as we watched them from inside the house. Every day they ate the food on the porch, played, chased bugs and butterflies in the backyard, and ran away when they saw us—even from afar.

One night when talking about "our" kittens I said, "I wonder if they ever think about where this food comes from. It just appears every day for them. I wish they knew we don't want to hurt them and just want to love them!"

Those words came back to me the next day when I was alone with my thoughts. I saw how we are so often like those little kittens. God is watching over us, loving us, and wanting us to trust and come to Him. He feeds us, provides for us, and uses so many situations to draw us close to Him. Like the kittens we come to the food and water, but if we see even a shadow of the Provider, we get scared and run away.

Our Provider is persistent and does not give up. Every day there are signs of His love calling us to come to Him. He looks forward to the day when we will allow Him to catch us and make us His own. That day we will be complete in Him and will have all that we ever need.

"And my God will supply every need of yours according to his riches in glory in Christ Jesus." (Philippians 4:19)

Reflection:

- Where or how have you seen God's provision?

- How is he calling you to Himself?

- Are you afraid? And if so, do you run away?

- Will you trust that He loves you and wants to make you His own?

DO I WANT
TO HELP?

My step-mother, Maxine, was once in a very bad financial situation and asked my husband, Ralph, for advice on how to resolve her crisis. He stepped in to help her and began explaining the truth of her situation so that she could best learn how to manage her finances. Maxine became irritated, and it became obvious that she didn't want advice on how to manage her finances or how to become financially secure; rather she wanted approval for the ways in which she had decided to manage her money. Ralph would not be able to help Maxine until she let him.

I began to compare this situation with how I often interact with God. There are times when I pray and ask God to help me. I know He has the answers to my problems. Am I willing to listen to His words, or do I just want what I want?

Do I just want God to approve of what I am doing? I have to ask myself whether I'm willing to be obedient and do what he says. Do I trust God to have my best interests at heart? Will I listen? Do I understand that God is just waiting to help me? Will

I listen and obey, or will I continue to do what I want and miss the opportunities God would provide for me.

Oh, dear God, Father, please help me to let You help me. Help me to open my heart to be obedient to your way for my life.

Forgive me for:

- not trusting you,

- not being willing to be obedient,

- and for wanting my way above Yours.

God has the answers to my problems. Will I listen to Him and be healed, or will I ignore Him and go my own way?

"Trust in the Lord with all your heart, and do not lean on your own understanding. In all your ways acknowledge him, and he will make straight your paths." (Proverbs 3:5–6)

LESSONS FROM DOG TRAINING

We welcomed a new puppy named Emma into our home. Like most puppies, Emma liked to chew on things, dig in the yard, and jump up on people and furniture. She was in desperate need of training, as her nature was to be wild and active. I enrolled her in dog-obedience school in the hope that it would change her habits and allow her to live in our home comfortably so we could fully enjoy being with her.

It occurred to me as I attended those classes with Emma that I am also born with an original nature that is wild and self-serving. At times I don't think God has my best interests at heart, so I do what I think is best for myself. God wants to open my eyes so I can see how wide and long and high and deep the love of Christ is for us (Ephesians 3:18).

He wants that love to draw me to Him and change my nature from being afraid or from rebelling to accepting and receiving His love. By trusting in God's love for me and obeying His commandments, God will change my heart, and changing my heart is what changes my nature so that I can trust and have fellowship with Him.

After realizing the ways in which I am like Emma, my prayer has been: "Please continue to mold and reshape me into what You would have me be."

"Do not be conformed to this world, but be transformed by the renewal of your mind, that by testing you may discern what is the will of God, what is good and acceptable and perfect." (Romans 12:2)

Reflection:

- Are you willing to allow God to change your nature from fear and rebellion to accepting and receiving His love for you?

- How have you been transformed by the renewing of your mind?

LET DOWN
YOUR SAILS

My husband and I had a Catalina-22 sailboat when we lived in Oklahoma and loved spending lazy days on Grand Lake with our family. Storms often popped up when we were on the lake and could quickly turn a beautiful day into a dangerous situation. My husband, an avid sailor, taught me to immediately let down the sails and turn the boat into the wind during a storm so that the boat would stop. Trying to fight the storm by keeping the sails up in those weather conditions would be dangerous at best—and potentially catastrophic.

I have encountered many storms in my life that have left me surrounded by confusion, not knowing which way to turn. I am often reminded in those moments of our sailing adventures, and I apply what I learned on our sailboat in the storms.

I need the strength and courage to let down my sails by letting go of trying to fight and control situations. Instead, I need to turn into the wind—God—and stop, allowing room for peace so that I can be led to safer ground.

Regarding this, God says, "Peace I leave with you; my peace I give to you. Not as the world gives do I give you. Let not your hearts be troubled, neither let them be afraid" (John 14:27).

Reflection:

- Where do you find peace and calm in the storms of your life?

Peace
I LEAVE WITH YOU;
MY PEACE I GIVE TO YOU.

Not as the world gives do I give you. LET NOT YOUR

BE TROUBLED
neither let them be afraid.

— John 14:27 —

THE GPS

I have become dependent on my car's GPS system. I input my destination and begin to drive the course as directed. I trust that the navigation system will guide me to my destination. When I miss a turn, the GPS will plot a new course to get me back on track and continue to lead me to my final destination.

Over the years I have come to trust in this artificial intelligence. Even at times when I didn't think my path looked right I was delighted to see that, even if it wasn't the route I would have chosen, I did end up where I wanted to be.

I was driving recently and realized that, just as I give my blind trust to the GPS navigation, God is my faithful and flawless GPS to eternal life. God has provided me with a map in the form of the Bible, and He speaks to me about where to go and what to do through prayer and scripture. "You shall love the Lord your God with all your heart and with all your soul and with all your mind" (Matthew 22:37).

As with anything, it is easy to get off track—and even go in the wrong direction. When I realize I am not following God's voice, I need to listen and turn my attention to hear Him say, "Trust Me."

John 14:6 says, "I am the way, and the truth, and the life. No one comes to the Father except through me." If I listen to and trust what God has taught me, I will quickly get back on track. No matter how many bad turns I make, God promises to redirect my steps and lead me to my eternal destination.

> Trust in the LORD with all your heart,
> and do not lean on your own
> understanding.
> In all your ways acknowledge him, and he will
> make
> straight your paths. (Proverbs 3:5–6)

Reflection:

- Are you allowing God to lead you and guide your path?

- Have you experienced getting off track and following God's word to get back where you want to go?

I AM
THE WAY
THE
Truth
AND THE
LIFE.

No one comes to the
Father except through me.

John 14:6

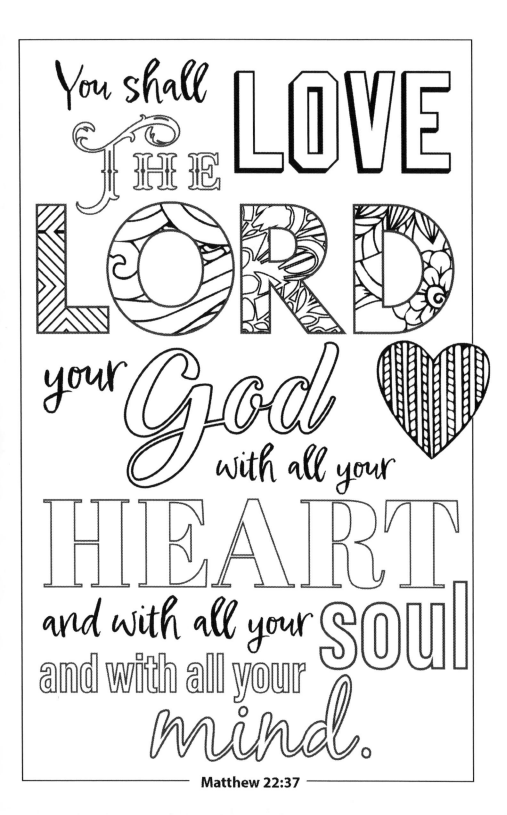

Matthew 22:37

EMAILS

Recently my husband and I were watching a television special about routine daily life aboard a naval vessel far from its home base.

A member of the crew shared how he looked forward to receiving an email from his wife every morning, which allowed them to stay connected. He remarked that some days the emails included long and detailed accounts from the day before while other days were just a quick check-in. Although the content and length of the emails changed from day to day, she would always:

- tell him how much she loved him,

- keep him in the loop of her life, and

- want him to feel connected to her and the family while he was so far away.

I was struck that this is similar to how I communicate with God. There are days when I find myself in constant dialogue with Him and others when I simply begin with a short prayer.

My prayers are not formal; rather, it is as though I am talking to a constant companion. I am not sharing myself in a one-sided relationship. Instead, through these check-ins, I hear Him whisper in my soul, and I remember His words of encouragement—that I am not alone, that He has a purpose for me, that I am loved, and that He is faithful.

This practice is not new. In fact, "And rising very early in the morning, while it was still dark, he departed and went out to a desolate place, and there he prayed" (Mark 1:35).

Jesus's need to check in was a simple affirmation of His love and intimate relationship with God the Father.

> Do not be anxious about anything, but in everything by prayer and supplication with thanksgiving let your requests be made known to God. And the peace of God, which surpasses all understanding, will guard your hearts and your minds in Christ Jesus. (Philippians 4:6-7)

Reflection:

- How can you remind yourself to connect with God daily through prayer?

- How will you start the conversation with God?

ROYALTY

President George W. and Laura Bush hosted Queen Elizabeth II of England at a state dinner in the White House. When I saw the pictures of the First Lady standing elegantly, welcoming the queen, I wondered if she could have ever imagined she would wind up in such a spot.

A few days later, as I sat quietly and spoke with God, I stopped and smiled to myself. *Who would have thought I would sit every morning and talk, cry, and laugh with the Creator of heaven and earth?* It's easy for me to put emphasis on people of royalty, celebrity, and power, but being with them cannot compare to the times I spend with God. I am blessed indeed!

> Have you not known?
> Have you not heard?
> The LORD is the everlasting God, the Creator of
> the ends of the earth.
> He does not faint or grow weary; his understanding
> is unsearchable. (Isaiah 40:28)

I was reminded in Psalm 16:11 that "You have made known to me the path of life; in your presence there is fullness of joy; at your right hand are pleasures forevermore."

Reflection:

- Have you ever set aside time when you can talk to God about what is on your heart?

- What is on your heart that you can discuss with God?

YOU HAVE MADE known to me the PATH OF LIFE; in your presence there is FULLNESS of JOY; at your right hand are pleasures forevermore.

Psalm 16:11

THE TEST

I attended real estate school when I lived in Louisiana. As my class prepared to take the final test, our teacher gave us smaller tests to prepare us for the *big* test. As he handed them out, he said, "A test is to let you know what you don't know."

His words have remained with me, and I have seen them be true in my spiritual life as well. The tests and trials I walk through are not meant to hurt me; rather, each test reveals what I have learned and what I still don't know.

With each test I ask myself:

- Do I trust God's purpose and love in the difficult times as well as the good?

- Do I remember to thank God each day for blessings large and small?

- Do I believe I can do all things through Christ who gives me strength? (Philippians 4:13)?

- Can I remember to "be strong and courageous Do not be afraid or terrified because of them for the LORD your

God goes with you; he will never leave you nor forsake you" (Deuteronomy 31:6)?

- Do I believe that my physical death is not the end of my life, but a continuation of eternal life through Jesus Christ?

I give them eternal life, and they shall never perish; no one will snatch them out of my hand" (John 10:28).

In the midst of my tests and trials, I ask God to lead me into a deeper relationship with Him.

"Blessed is the man who remains steadfast under trial, for when he has stood the test he will receive the crown of life, which God has promised to those who love him" (James 1:12).

Reflection:

- Do you trust God's promises during the tests?

- What are some of God's promises that you can hold on to when you experience trials?

I CAN DO ALL THINGS THROUGH *Christ* WHO GIVES ME STRENGTH.

Philippians 4:13

THE VACUUM CLEANER

I enjoy listening to music on my headphones while cleaning my house. One day as I was vacuuming the carpet, I noticed something had happened. I was still moving the vacuum cleaner back and forth, but it wasn't picking anything up. I took my headphones off to realize that I no longer heard the noise of the vacuum. I looked around and saw the vacuum cleaner had come unplugged.

Immediately it all made sense. When it was plugged in, the vacuum cleaner did what it was designed to. When it came unplugged, it was just a useless object I moved back and forth.

In that moment it became clear that God is the One with the power. He allows me to be the expression of that power, but I must remember it belongs to God. Through Him I can do all the things I was created for.

John 15:5 paints a beautiful word picture by saying, "I am the vine, you are the branches. Whoever abides in me and I in him, he it is that bears much fruit, for apart from me you can do nothing."

Reflection:

- Think about the example of the vacuum cleaner, what does it mean to you to be connected to God?

- If you feel unconnected, what can you do to be connected again?

I AM THE VINE, YOU ARE THE branches. Whoever abides in me and I in him, he it is that bears much fruit, for apart from me you can do nothing.

John 15:5

WEIGHT
WATCHERS

I had a bit of a weight problem as a teenager. I loved cookies, cake, and candy, as well as all other carbohydrates because they were so good! I didn't really worry about it when I began to gain weight and continued to eat everything I liked. Food was such a comfort to me.

When I realized my weight was a problem, I tried to find ways to lose it. I tried all kinds of diets as a quick fix, but fundamentally, I didn't want to change my lifestyle. I wanted the weight to go away by itself. My husband ran every day and went to the gym, but I didn't feel like exercising; I rationalized that I didn't have time.

I finally realized that if I really wanted to lose weight, I would have to concentrate and focus on doing what I needed to do, so I joined Weight Watchers. I went to the meetings, I counted points, I prayed, I wrote down everything I ate, I exercised, and I thought about my goal. I began to lose weight, and it felt wonderful. I ended up losing twenty pounds.

After a while I quit following the rules and began to gain the weight back again. Then I remembered what I needed to do and began my healthy eating habits and exercising once again. It is easy for me to slip and go back to bad habits, but now I know what to do when I get off track.

This is very similar to my spiritual walk with Christ. For many years I lived my life with no particular purpose or plan. I had heard about having abundant life in Christ, but I didn't know what that looked like or how to live it. However, in 1988 I was given the opportunity to attend a retreat where I heard and saw what a life centered in Jesus Christ looked like, and I wanted that life!

I learned that this new life centered on knowing God, trusting Jesus for my salvation, and believing that the Holy Spirit will guide and direct my life on a day-by-day basis.

The more I read and studied the Bible, the more I could hear the quiet voice of God teaching me His ways. I have found fellowship in the church, small groups, Bible studies, and friends from all over the country who share what they have learned and listen to what is happening in my life. They have become my dearest friends.

As I have walked in this new life, I have had times of following the plan and seeing God working in my life. I have also had times of wandering away from the plan and realizing I have lost my way. In all of it, I know that God knows exactly where I am all the time, and He allows circumstances and my desire to know Him to lead me back to Him.

My constant prayer is that I will desire with all my heart to stay close to the Good Shepherd and not wander off. "Return to the LORD your God, for he is gracious and merciful, slow to anger, and abounding in steadfast love; and he relents over disaster" (Joel 2:13).

Reflection:

- What experiences or circumstances in your life have let you know you need to return to the Lord?

- Write a prayer telling God how you have gotten off track, and ask for His grace to lead you back to Him.

PREPARING

Our family has begun a tradition of meeting together in Florida for a week in February. I look forward to it every year. This year we have decided to spend a week in Orlando and to visit Disney World. I began planning for this trip in June because I wanted it to be just right.

I was overwhelmed by all the options Disney and other Orlando parks had to offer. I purchased a travel book to help me navigate the many offerings and created a plan for how we wanted to spend our time together. I spent weeks looking for the perfect house to rent and spoke to my daughters about the meals we would prepare together and other additions that would make our time together special. Planning and preparing brings me great joy, and then when we are together, I don't have to worry so much about details and can enjoy being with my family.

While preparing this trip I realized that God loves to prepare as well and has been preparing for all of us from the beginning of time. John 1:1–3 says, "In the beginning was the Word, and the Word was with God, and the Word was God. He was with God in the beginning. All things were created through him, and apart from him not one thing was created that has been created." God prepared the perfect place for us to live. He provided everything that was needed for His creation to live and thrive.

When we went astray and rebelled (and we have *all* gone astray and rebelled), God prepared a way back from our sin in to a relationship with Him. He prepared Jesus for us. "For all have sinned and fall short of the glory of God" (Romans 3:23). Romans 5:6–8 reminds us, "For while we were still weak, at the right time Christ died for the ungodly. For one will scarcely die for a righteous person-- though perhaps for a good person one would dare even to die but God shows his love for us in that while we were still sinners, Christ died for us."

In Jesus, God prepared a way for us to live with Him forever. That is, we will live beyond our physical death. John 3:16 says, "For God so loved the world, that he gave his only Son, that whoever believes in him should not perish but have eternal life."

One of our greatest fears is that of the unknown. We don't know what will happen to us when we die. Is it over? Is this all there is? Jesus knows our fears and gives us words of comfort. He reminds us to, "Let not your hearts be troubled. Believe in God; believe also in me. In my Father's house are many rooms. If it were not so, would I have told you that I go to prepare a place for you? And if I go and prepare a place for you, I will come again and take you to myself, that where I am you may be also" (John 1:1–3).

From the beginning of time to forever, God has prepared, is preparing, and will prepare for us. He does this for us because of his great *love.*

Reflection:

- Remember a time when you prepared something special for someone.

What was it like? How did you feel?

- How does it make you feel to know God has prepared for you since the beginning of time to forever?

For God so loved the world, that he gave his only Son, that whoever BELIEVES IN HIM SHOULD NOT PERISH BUT HAVE ETERNAL Life.

John 3:16

Printed in the United States
by Baker & Taylor Publisher Services